NOW EVERY KID CAN WIN AT READING!

Sight words, also called high-frequency words, are the words that appear most often in the grade-level books your child is reading. While some high-frequency words are only a few letters long, they usually break the rules when it comes to spelling and can be difficult to "sound out." Kids who learn to recognize these words by sight enjoy greater reading success and increased fluency.

The Incredible Sight Word Workbook for Minecrafters uses Frye's list of high-frequency sight words plus exciting Minecraft-themed illustrations and sentences to make reading practice fun. Introduce a new word each day to build your child's confidence and increase their vocabulary. With over 100 gamer-friendly practice pages and puzzles for re___ child will be eager to advance their learni___ up their reading skills.

and

Trace the word below. Say the word as you trace it.

and and and and and

Finish the sentence. Write the word on the line.

Zombie jumps _____ plays.

Circle the correct word:

and	ant	an	ask	are

Build the word using Minecraft blocks.

Example:

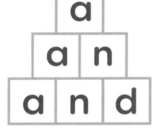

Now you try:

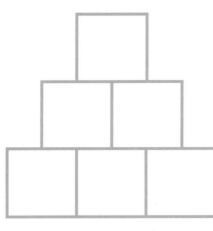

THE INCREDIBLE SIGHT WORD WORKBOOK FOR

100+ Fun Learning Activities to Boost Reading Skills

An Unofficial Activity Book for Minecrafters

Illustrated by
Grace Sandford

Sky Pony Press
New York

Copyright © 2022 by Hollan Publishing, Inc.

Minecraft® is a registered trademark of Notch Development AB.

The Minecraft game is copyright © Mojang AB.

All rights reserved. No part of this book may be reproduced in any manner without the express written consent of the publisher, except in the case of brief excerpts in critical reviews or articles. All inquiries should be addressed to Sky Pony Press, 307 West 36th Street, 11th Floor, New York, NY 10018.

Sky Pony Press books may be purchased in bulk at special discounts for sales promotion, corporate gifts, fund-raising, or educational purposes. Special editions can also be created to specifications. For details, contact the Special Sales Department, Sky Pony Press, 307 West 36th Street, 11th Floor, New York, NY 10018 or info@skyhorsepublishing.com.

Sky Pony® is a registered trademark of Skyhorse Publishing, Inc.®, a Delaware corporation.

Visit our website at www.skyponypress.com.

10 9 8 7 6 5 4 3 2 1

Library of Congress Cataloging-in-Publication Data is available on file.

Cover and interior artwork by Grace Sandford

Book design by Noora Cox

Print ISBN: 978-1-5107-6915-1

Printed in China

be

Trace the word below. Say the word as you trace it.

be be be be be

Finish the sentence. Write the word on the line.

Minecraft can _____ super fun.

Circle the correct word:

bed   but   do   bee   be

Draw a picture of something else that's fun.

can

Trace the word below. Say the word as you trace it.

can   can   can   can   can

Finish the sentence. Write the word on the line.

He _____ brush his teeth.

Circle the correct word:

an   **car**   **can**

and   **cat**

Solve the maze and make a sight word.

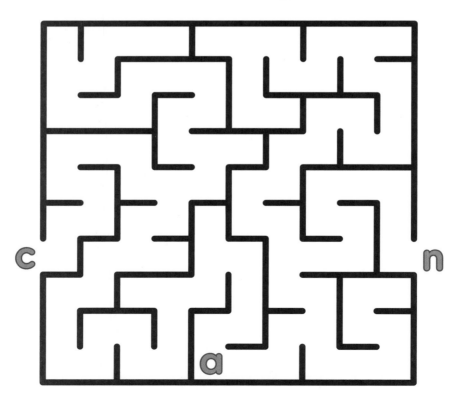

down

Trace the word below. Say the word as you trace it.

down   down   down   down

Finish the sentence. Write the word on the line.

The minecart goes _____ the hill.

Circle the correct word:

down   **do**   **does**   **don**   **own**

Draw your favorite Minecraft items in the minecart.

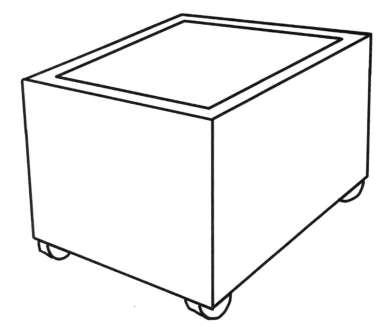

the

Trace the word below. Say the word as you trace it.

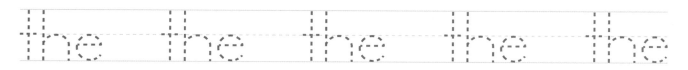

Finish the sentence. Write the word on the line.

Shoot _____ arrow at the mob.

Circle the correct word:

teh   tee   the   rhe   thee

Build the word using Minecraft blocks.

Example:

Now you try:

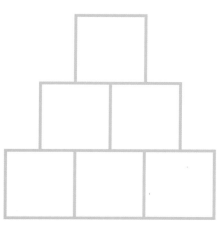 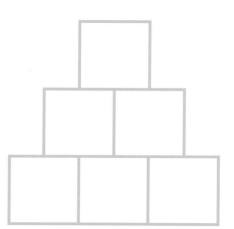

people

Trace the word below. Say the word as you trace it.

Finish the sentence. Write the word on the line.

Silverfish attack _____ .

Circle the correct word:

poppy   pickle   poeple

people   peeple

Connect the dots to make the first letter of **people**.

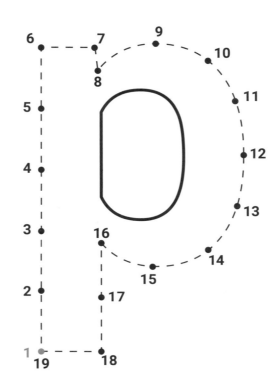

for

Trace the word below. Say the word as you trace it.

Finish the sentence. Write the word on the line.

I mine _____ diamonds.

Circle the correct word:

for   four   fot   tor   fur

Draw something you like to mine for.

I

Trace the word below. Say the word as you trace it.

I   I   I   I   I

Finish the sentence. Write the word on the line.

_____ can ride a llama.

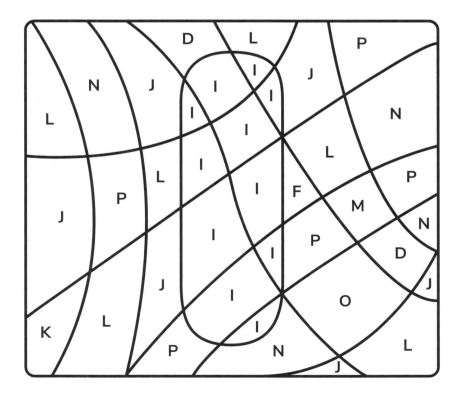

Circle the correct word:

Y   L   T

    I   J

Color the spaces with I to make the word.

that

Trace the word below. Say the word as you trace it.

that   that   that   that

Finish the sentence. Write the word on the line.

I want _____ diamond sword.

Circle the correct word:

thet   than   that   tat   thath

Solve the maze and make a sight word.

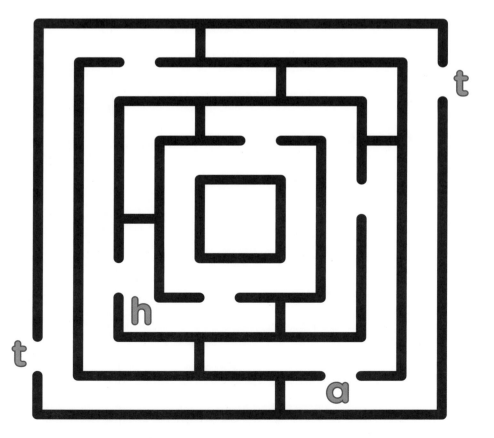

was

Trace the word below. Say the word as you trace it.

was   was   was   was   was

Finish the sentence. Write the word on the line.

The sun _____ hot.

Circle the correct word:

wuzz   **wass**   **wus**

     was   **waz**

Connect the dots to make the first letter of **was**.

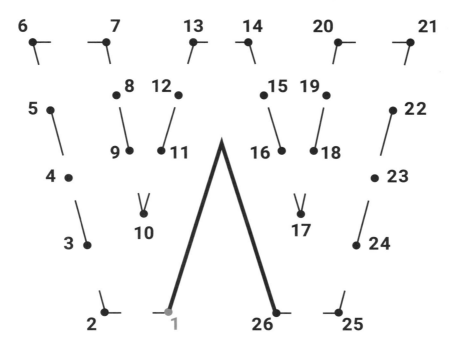

or

Trace the word below. Say the word as you trace it.

or or or or or

Finish the sentence. Write the word on the line.

I can read _____ I can play.

Circle the correct word:

or   ohr   over   oar   orr

Build the word using Minecraft blocks.

Example:

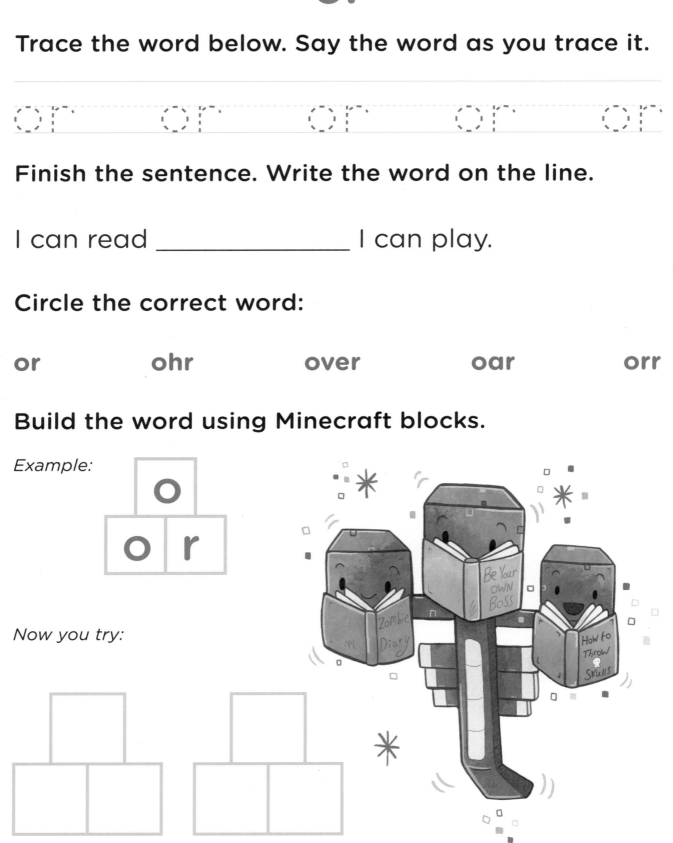

o

o r

Now you try:

of

Trace the word below. Say the word as you trace it.

of   of   of   of   of

Finish the sentence. Write the word on the line.

I have an Eye _____ Ender.

Circle the correct word:

uf   af   of   uv   off

Draw a picture of something found in The End.

one

Trace the word below. Say the word as you trace it.

one one one one one

Finish the sentence. Write the word on the line.

He has _____ dog.

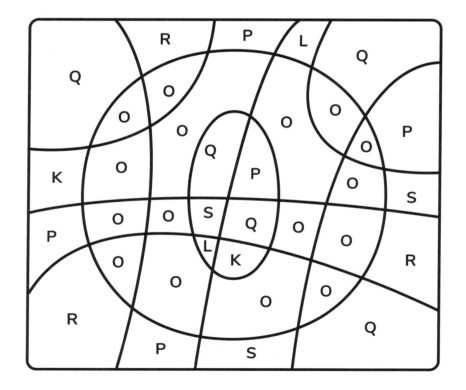

Circle the correct word:

wun   oen   on

onn   one

Color the spaces where you see the first letter of **one**.

had

Trace the word below. Say the word as you trace it.

had had had had had

Finish the sentence. Write the word on the line.

We _____ to go.

Circle the correct word:

hid   had   hed   hat   hadd

Build the word using Minecraft blocks.

Example:

Now you try:

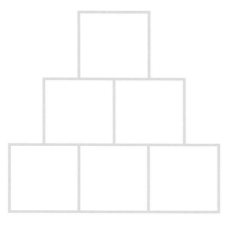
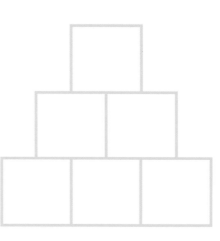

a

Trace the word below. Say the word as you trace it.

Finish the sentence. Write the word on the line.

The villager has _____ gem.

Circle the correct word:

ay   ai   ah

      e   a

Solve the maze and make a sight word.

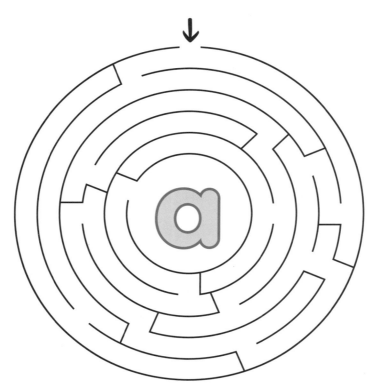

by

Trace the word below. Say the word as you trace it.

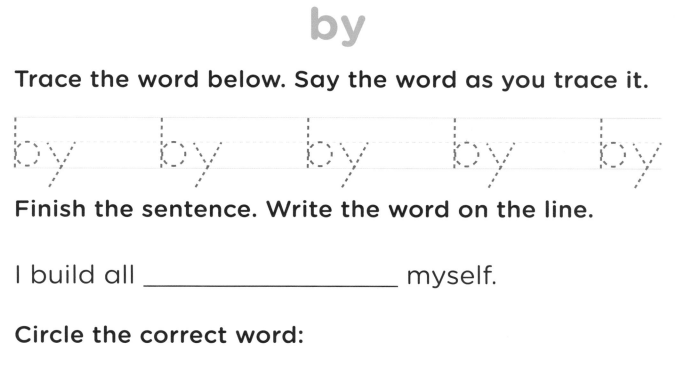

by   by   by   by   by

Finish the sentence. Write the word on the line.

I build all _____ myself.

Circle the correct word:

by   **byy**   **byu**   **bj**   **bi**

Draw something you can do by yourself.

17

words

Trace the word below. Say the word as you trace it.

words   words   words

Finish the sentence. Write the word on the line.

Read the _____

on the sign.

Circle the correct word:

words   wurds   word

worrds   wordz

Fill this space with words from the game of Minecraft.

in

Trace the word below. Say the word as you trace it.

in in in in in

Finish the sentence. Write the word on the line.

The potion is _____ the bottle.

Circle the correct word:

in   inn   ing   im   ih

Draw the rest of the picture. Color the potion in the bottle.

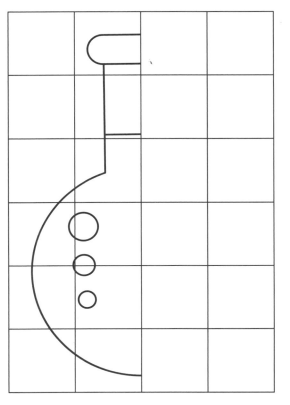

but

Trace the word below. Say the word as you trace it.

but   but   but   but   but

Finish the sentence. Write the word on the line.

Endermites are small _____ dangerous.

Circle the correct word:

buf   bat   bot   but   butt

Build the word using Minecraft blocks.

Example:

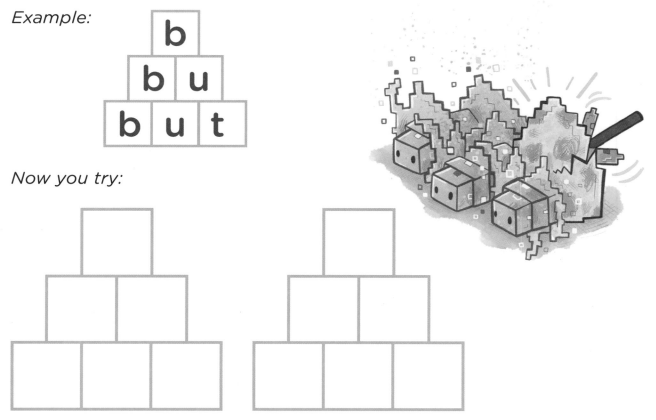

Now you try:

is

Trace the word below. Say the word as you trace it.

Finish the sentence. Write the word on the line.

The zombie _____ mad.

Circle the correct word:

iz   iss   his   ys   is

Solve the maze and make a sight word.

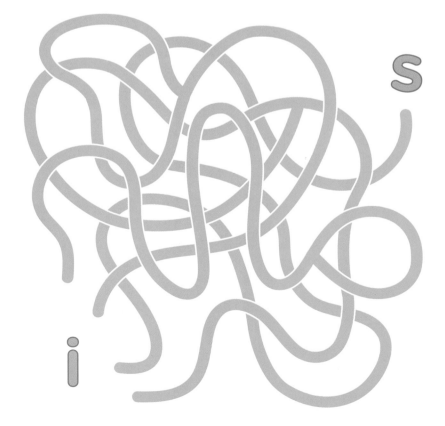

not

Trace the word below. Say the word as you trace it.

not   not   not   not   not

Finish the sentence. Write the word on the line.

A ghast is _____ friendly.

Circle the correct word:

nott   **nut**   **not**

     knot   **noot**

Connect the dots to see the gaming object.

you

Trace the word below. Say the word as you trace it.

you   you   you   you   you

Finish the sentence. Write the word on the line.

_____ can dig to find a cave.

Circle the correct word:

yoo   **yo**   **you**   **wou**   **yu**

Trace and color the shovel for digging in Minecraft.

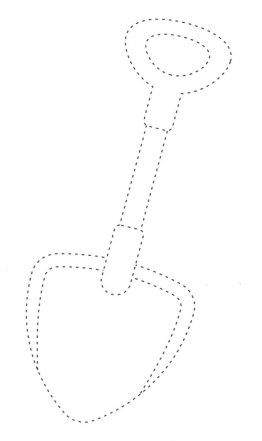

what

Trace the word below. Say the word as you trace it.

what   what   what   what

Finish the sentence. Write the word on the line.

I know _____ to build.

Circle the correct word:

what   **wat**   **whut**   **wath**   **want**

Solve the maze and make a sight word.

24

to

Trace the word below. Say the word as you trace it.

Finish the sentence. Write the word on the line.

Try _____ catch a fish.

Circle the correct word:

two   ta   to

     tu   too

Draw a picture of a fish you catch in Minecraft.

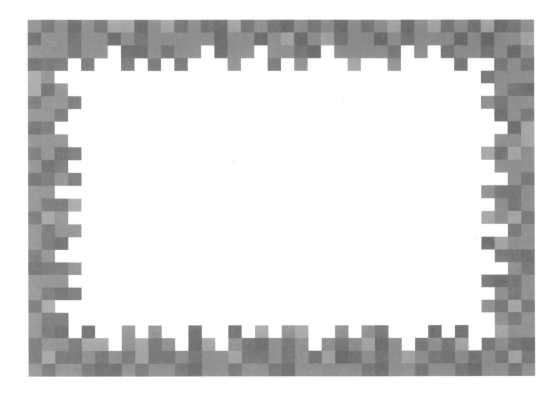

all

Trace the word below. Say the word as you trace it.

Finish the sentence. Write the word on the line.

I mined _____ the gold.

Circle the correct word:

al   all   oll   aul   awl

Build the word using Minecraft blocks.

Example:

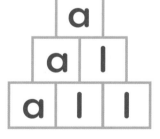

Now you try:

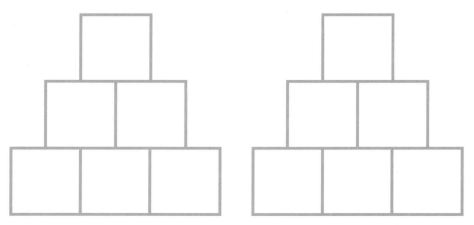

it

Trace the word below. Say the word as you trace it.

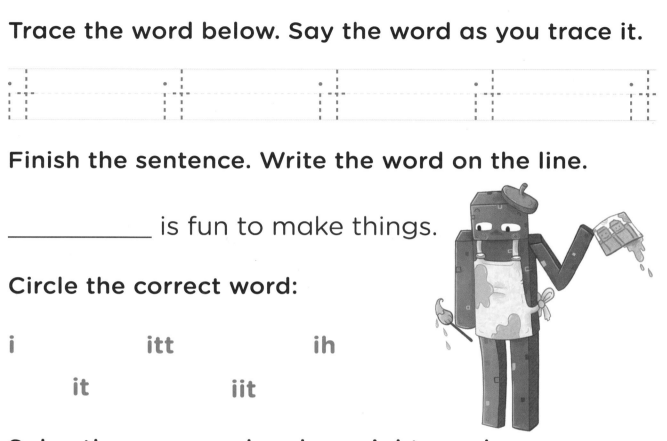

Finish the sentence. Write the word on the line.

_____ is fun to make things.

Circle the correct word:

i   itt   ih

    it   iit

Solve the maze and make a sight word.

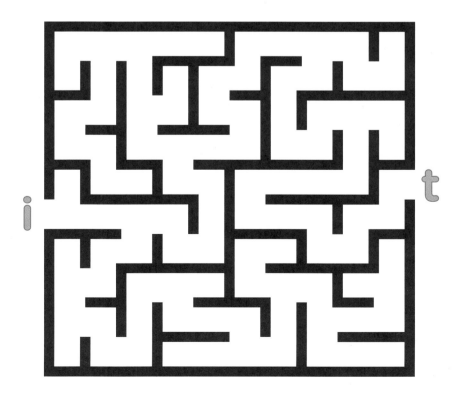

were

Trace the word below. Say the word as you trace it.

were were were were

Finish the sentence. Write the word on the line.

The guardians _____ chasing me.

Circle the correct word:

wer   was   where   were   wur

Connect the dots to make a gaming device, then color it in!

28

he

Trace the word below. Say the word as you trace it.

Finish the sentence. Write the word on the line.

Steve gets wood so _____ can make a bed.

Circle the correct word:

hee　　　　**she**　　　　**he**　　　　**hy**　　　　**her**

Draw the items you need to make a bed in Minecraft.

we

Trace the word below. Say the word as you trace it.

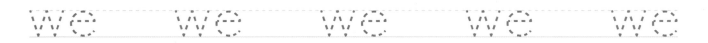

we   we   we   we   we

Finish the sentence. Write the word on the line.

I like how _____

work together.

Circle the correct word:

whe   wer   wee

we   why

Draw you and a friend in the overworld.

when

Trace the word below. Say the word as you trace it.

when   when   when   when

Finish the sentence. Write the word on the line.

It's usually dark _____ zombies attack.

Circle the correct word:

when   wenn   wher   whem   wen

Build the word using Minecraft blocks.

Example:

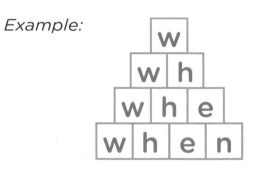

Now you try:

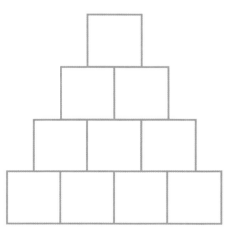   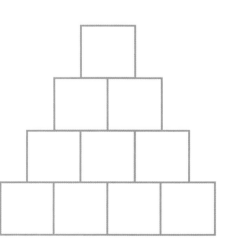

your

Trace the word below. Say the word as you trace it.

your   your   your   your

Finish the sentence. Write the word on the line.

Put _____ items in a chest.

Circle the correct word:

yor   yoor   your

    yur   yore

Connect the dots to make the first
letter of **your**.

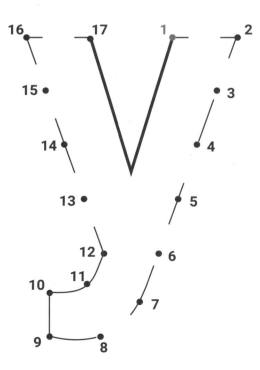

on

Trace the word below. Say the word as you trace it.

on   on   on   on   on

Finish the sentence. Write the word on the line.

Make the potion _____ the brewing stand.

Circle the correct word:

onn   **oh**   **on**   **an**   **un**

Solve the maze and make a sight word.

n

o

are

Trace the word below. Say the word as you trace it.

are   are   are   are   are

Finish the sentence. Write the word on the line.

Cave spiders _____ scary.

Circle the correct word:

are   **our**   **ore**

    ar   **arr**

Circle the two spider webs that are the same.

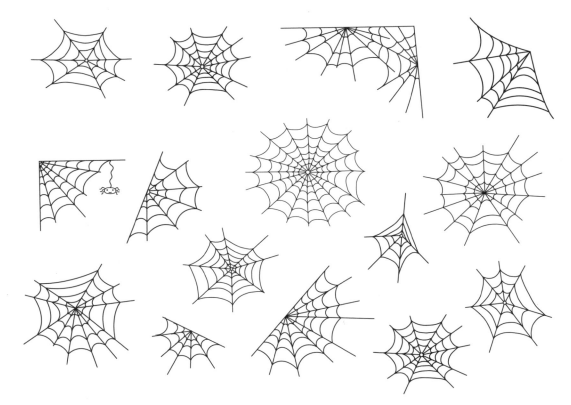

said

Trace the word below. Say the word as you trace it.

said   said   said   said

Finish the sentence. Write the word on the line.

He _____ to shoot at the End crystals.

Circle the correct word:

sead   **sayd**   **said**   **sait**   **sed**

Draw the Ender Dragon below.

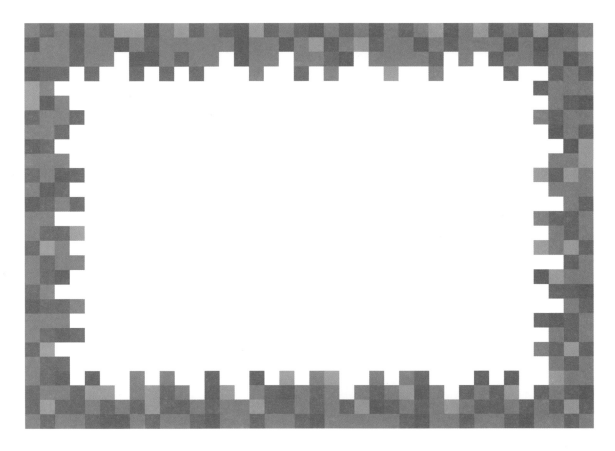

as

Trace the word below. Say the word as you trace it.

Finish the sentence. Write the word on the line.

Run _____ fast as you can.

Circle the correct word:

as   **az**   **ais**

      ase   **sas**

Connect the dots to make the first
letter of **as**.

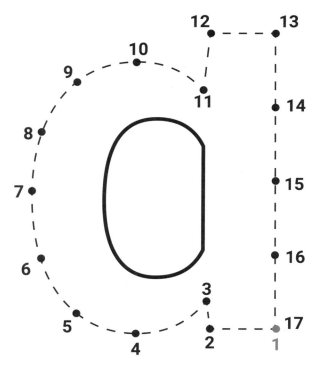

there

Trace the word below. Say the word as you trace it.

there there there there

Finish the sentence. Write the word on the line.

Put the TNT over _____ .

Circle the correct word:

then   tere   there   ther   her

Circle the TNT block.

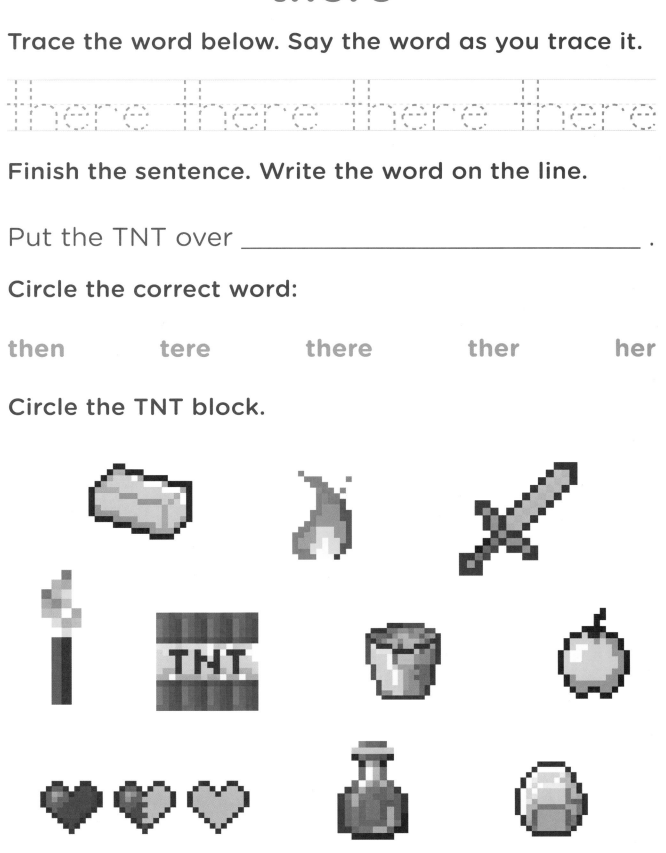

with

Trace the word below. Say the word as you trace it.

with with with with with

Finish the sentence. Write the word on the line.

You can teleport _____ chorus fruit.

Circle the correct word:

wit   wish   with   wint   witch

Build the word using Minecraft blocks.

Example:

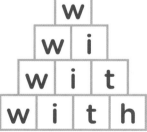

Now you try:

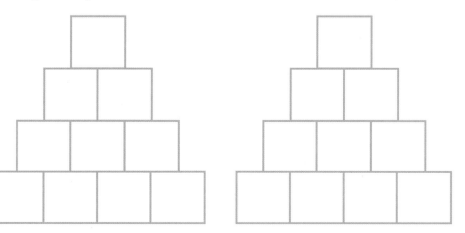

use

Trace the word below. Say the word as you trace it.

use   use   use   use   use

Finish the sentence. Write the word on the line.

You can _____ gold to trade with piglins.

Circle the correct word:

us   eus   yuse

    use   ues

Color the piglin's sword gold.

his

Trace the word below. Say the word as you trace it.

his   his   his   his   his

Finish the sentence. Write the word on the line.

Steve uses _____

skeleton spawner.

Circle the correct word:

hiss   hiz   hiis

      his   hits

Solve the maze and make a sight word.

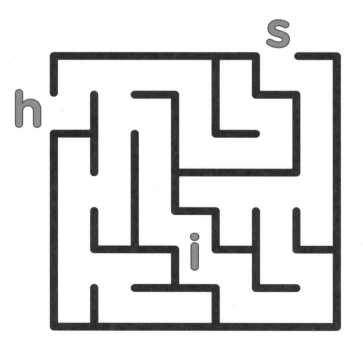

an

Trace the word below. Say the word as you trace it.

an   an   an   an   an

Finish the sentence. Write the word on the line.

Use _____ Eye of Ender to find a stronghold.

Circle the correct word:

un   an   and   ann   na

Draw an Eye of Ender just like this one!

they

Trace the word below. Say the word as you trace it.

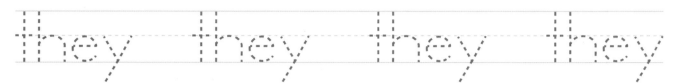

they   they   they   they

Finish the sentence. Write the word on the line.

The zombie villagers are happy

that _____ are cured!

Circle the correct word:

the   then   tey

      them   they

Connect the dots and color this golden cure for zombie villagers!

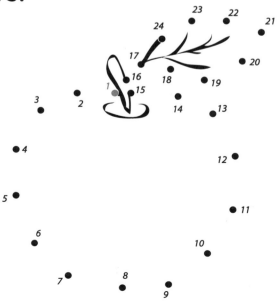

each

Trace the word below. Say the word as you trace it.

each   each   each   each

Finish the sentence. Write the word on the line.

I use _____ weapon in my inventory.

Circle the correct word:

ech   eecg   each   eash   eich

Build the word using Minecraft blocks.

Example:

e			
e	a		
e	a	c	
e	a	c	h

Now you try:

which

Trace the word below. Say the word as you trace it.

which which which which

Finish the sentence. Write the word on the line.

Tell me _____

potion makes me strong.

Circle the correct word:

wich   with   whic

which   witch

Circle the fire resistance potion in the group of objects below.

at

Trace the word below. Say the word as you trace it.

at   at   at   at   at

Finish the sentence. Write the word on the line.

Meet me _____ the desert temple.

Circle the correct word:

ai   ath   art   af   at

Draw a desert temple below.

she

Trace the word below. Say the word as you trace it.

she   she   she   she   she

Finish the sentence. Write the word on the line.

That's the sword _____

uses the most.

Circle the correct word:

see   she   sha

     sea   he

Solve the maze and make a sight word.

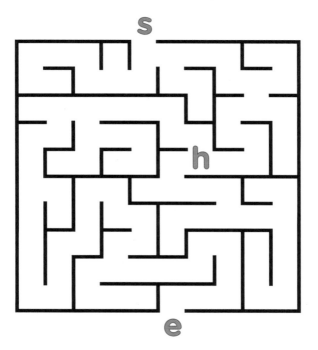

do

Trace the word below. Say the word as you trace it.

do   do   do   do   do

Finish the sentence. Write the word on the line.

You _____ not want to stare at an Enderman.

Circle the correct word:

doo   **doe**   **bo**   **do**   **du**

Which one is an Enderman? Circle it.

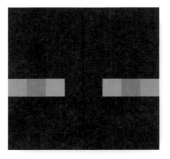
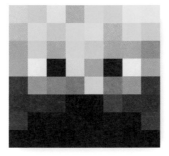

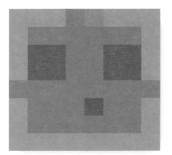
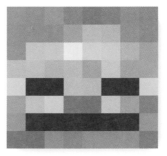

this

Trace the word below. Say the word as you trace it.

this this this this this

Finish the sentence. Write the word on the line.

An iron golem protects

_____ village.

Circle the correct word:

the   then   this

thin   thic

Color the flower that an iron golem might give to a villager.

48

how

Trace the word below. Say the word as you trace it.

how how how how how

Finish the sentence. Write the word on the line.

I know _____ to enchant a pickaxe.

Circle the correct word:

how   hou   hov   haw   howe

Color the pickaxe and write the name of your favorite enchantment.

This pickaxe is enchanted with: _____

have

Trace the word below. Say the word as you trace it.

have   have   have   have

Finish the sentence. Write the word on the line.

Guardians _____ spikes on their bodies.

Circle the correct word:

half   hav   heve   hawe   have

Build the word using Minecraft blocks.

Example:

Now you try:

their

Trace the word below. Say the word as you trace it.

their   their   their   their

Finish the sentence. Write the word on the line.

Alex and Steve use a compass to find

_____ way home.

Circle the correct word:

theyr   their   thier   thair   teir

Color the picture of the compass.

from

Trace the word below. Say the word as you trace it.

Finish the sentence. Write the word on the line.

Run away _____ hostile mobs.

Circle the correct word:

fram   **frum**   **fom**   **from**   **fromm**

Draw a picture of a hostile mob in Minecraft.

Trace the word below. Say the word as you trace it.

if   if   if   if   if

Finish the sentence. Write the word on the line.

Follow a dolphin _____ you want treasure.

Circle the correct word:

of   iff   iv

     af   if

Solve the maze and make a sight word.

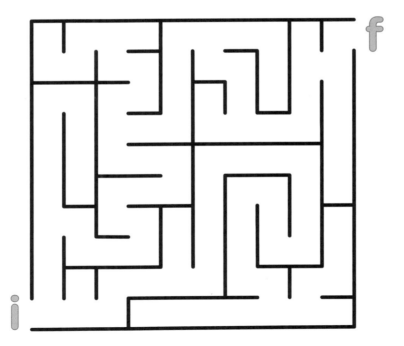

will

Trace the word below. Say the word as you trace it.

will   will   will   will   will

Finish the sentence. Write the word on the line.

A spider _____ not attack in Creative mode.

Circle the correct word:

wilk   **wil**   **will**   **wall**   **well**

Build the word using Minecraft blocks.

Example:

Now you try:

number

Trace the word below. Say the word as you trace it.

number number number

Finish the sentence. Write the word on the line.

Count the _____ of wood blocks you have.

Circle the correct word:

numbar   mumber   number   nuber   bumber

Color by number to create a Minecraft creature.

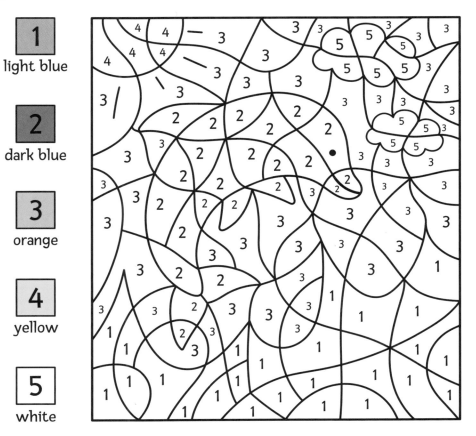

1 light blue

2 dark blue

3 orange

4 yellow

5 white

up

Trace the word below. Say the word as you trace it.

up   up   up   up   up

Finish the sentence. Write the word on the line.

You can blow _____

a house with TNT blocks.

Circle the correct word:

upp   op   ub

up   ap

Cut the picture out and fold it into a Minecraft TNT block.

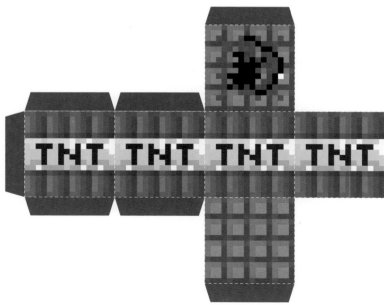

no

Trace the word below. Say the word as you trace it.

no   no   no   no   no

Finish the sentence. Write the word on the line.

There is _____ light in this cave.

Circle the correct word:

nou   noo   mo   nuo   no

Connect the dots to make an animal you see in a cave.

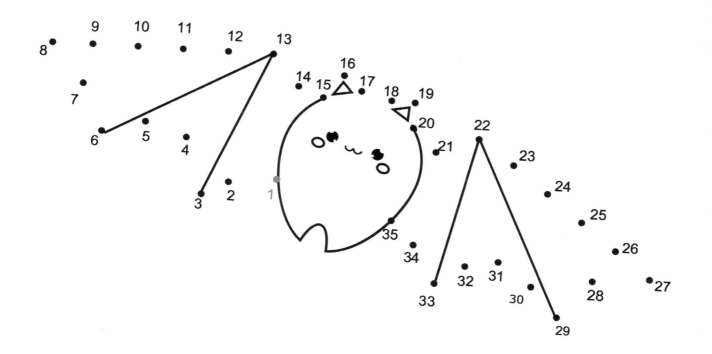

other

Trace the word below. Say the word as you trace it.

Finish the sentence. Write the word on the line.

Watch out for the _____

skeleton behind you!

Circle the correct word:

othr   other   otter

ofher   ather

Draw the other half of the skeleton.

way

Trace the word below. Say the word as you trace it.

way way way way way

Finish the sentence. Write the word on the line.

This is the _____ back to our base!

Circle the correct word:

wai   wav   yay   waa   way

Build the word using Minecraft blocks.

Example:

w
w	a
w	a	y

Now you try:

about

Trace the word below. Say the word as you trace it.

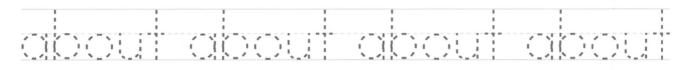

Finish the sentence. Write the word on the line.

I know all _____

fighting the Ender Dragon!

Circle the correct word:

aboot   abowt   about

ubout   ebout

Color the hatched dragon egg.

could

Trace the word below. Say the word as you trace it.

Finish the sentence. Write the word on the line.

You _____ build a mob farm.

Circle the correct word:

culd   cold   could   choud   cood

Connect the dots to make the first letter of could.

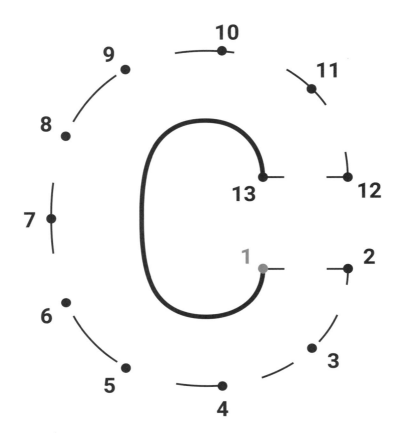

out

Trace the word below. Say the word as you trace it.

out   out   out   out   out

Finish the sentence. Write the word on the line.

There are hostile mobs

_____ there!

Circle the correct word:

outh   owt   ot

    uot   out

Solve the maze and make a sight word.

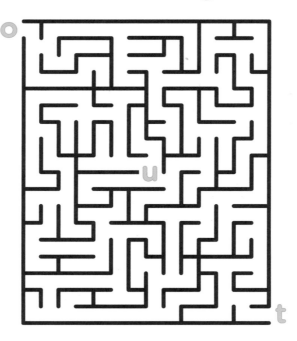

these

Trace the word below. Say the word as you trace it.

these these these these

Finish the sentence. Write the word on the line.

I use _____ trap doors to catch zombies.

Circle the correct word:

thees   thes   these   the   this

Draw a trap for catching zombies below.

many

Trace the word below. Say the word as you trace it.

many   many   many   many

Finish the sentence. Write the word on the line.

Minecraft sheep come in _____ colors.

Circle the correct word:

meny   many   manny   money   nany

Build the word using Minecraft blocks.

Example:

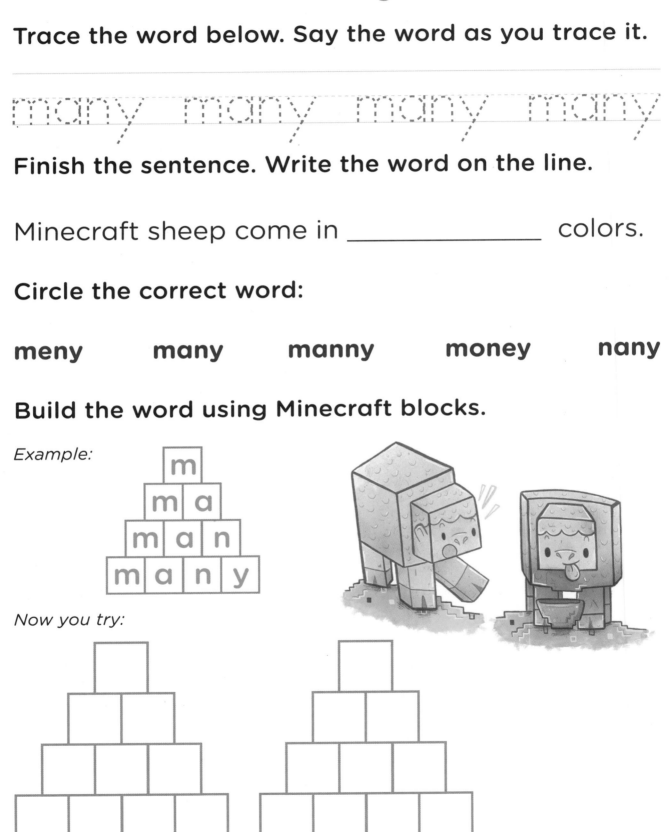

Now you try:

my

Trace the word below. Say the word as you trace it.

my   my   my   my   my

Finish the sentence. Write the word on the line.

I place _____ torch on the cave wall.

Circle the correct word:

my   **mi**   **me**   **ny**   **mye**

Help Steve and his dog find the torch.

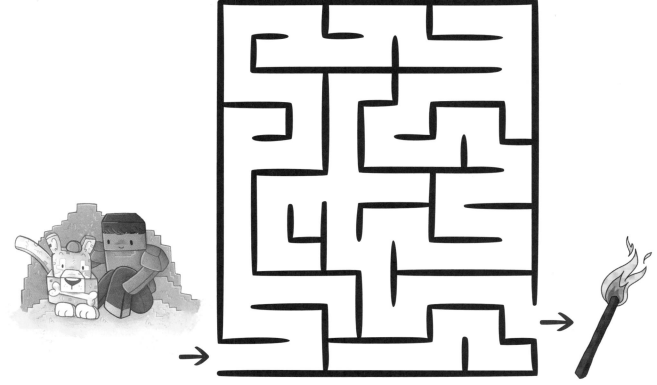

then

Trace the word below. Say the word as you trace it.

then   then   then   then

Finish the sentence. Write the word on the line.

Wait for the shulker box to

open, _____ attack.

Circle the correct word:

than   **the**   **theen**

thet   **then**

Copy the picture to add another heart to your health bar.

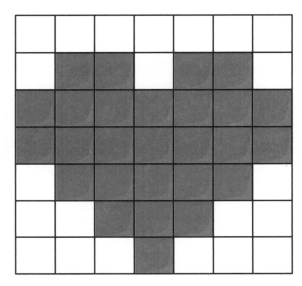

66

first

Trace the word below. Say the word as you trace it.

first   first   first   first

Finish the sentence. Write the word on the line.

I survived the _____ night in Minecraft.

Circle the correct word:

fist   fire   firth   first   forst

Connect the dots to make the first letter of first.

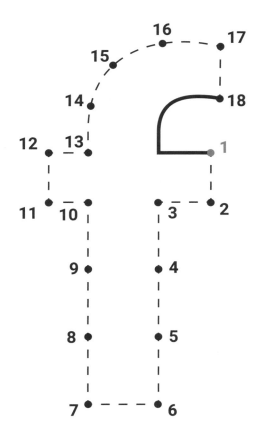

water

Trace the word below. Say the word as you trace it.

Finish the sentence. Write the word on the line.

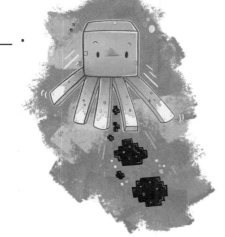

Squids live in the _____ .

Circle the correct word:

waiter   water   wather

weter   watter

Draw a Minecraft creature that lives in the water.

than

Trace the word below. Say the word as you trace it.

than　　than　　than　　than

Finish the sentence. Write the word on the line.

I have more redstone _____ you.

Circle the correct word:

then　　　　**thenn**　　　　**than**　　　　**that**　　　　**them**

Build the word using Minecraft blocks.

Example:

Now you try:

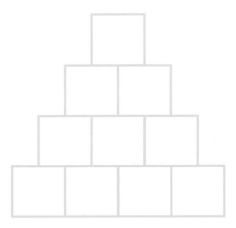
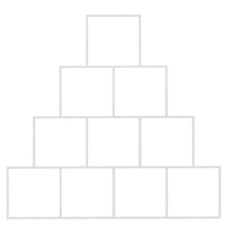

them

Trace the word below. Say the word as you trace it.

them them them them

Finish the sentence. Write the word on the line.

I can tame _____ with food.

Circle the correct word:

them   **theme**   **then**

themm   **they**

Color the fish you can use to tame a stray cat in Minecraft.

SO

Trace the word below. Say the word as you trace it.

SO   SO   SO   SO   SO   SO

Finish the sentence. Write the word on the line.

I am _____ mad at that griefer!

Circle the correct word:

so   sou   sew   si   soo

Solve the maze and make a sight word.

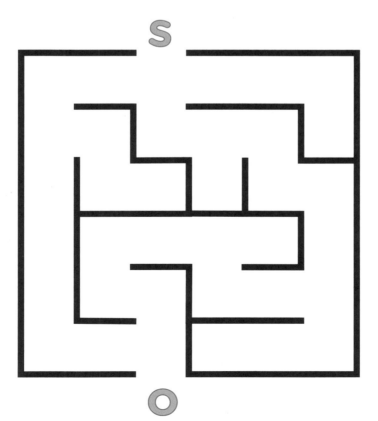

been

Trace the word below. Say the word as you trace it.

been   been   been   been

Finish the sentence. Write the word on the line.

The rabbit has _____

eating carrots.

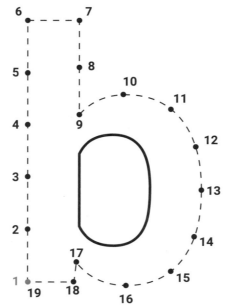

Circle the correct word:

bene   bean   bein

    bin   been

Connect the dots to make the first
letter of **been**.

some

Trace the word below. Say the word as you trace it.

some   some   some   some

Finish the sentence. Write the word on the line.

I can grow _____ pumpkins on my farm.

Circle the correct word:

sum   som   some   soom   soma

Build the word using Minecraft blocks.

Example:

Now you try:

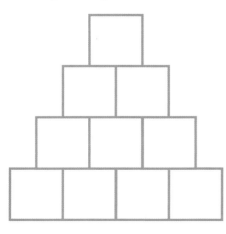 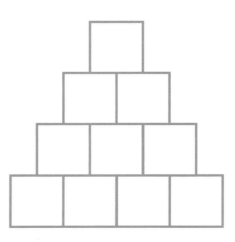

called

Trace the word below. Say the word as you trace it.

called called called called

Finish the sentence. Write the word on the line.

The mob _____

out for help.

Circle the correct word:

caled   calld   call

called   calt

Cut the picture out and fold it into a Minecraft chest.

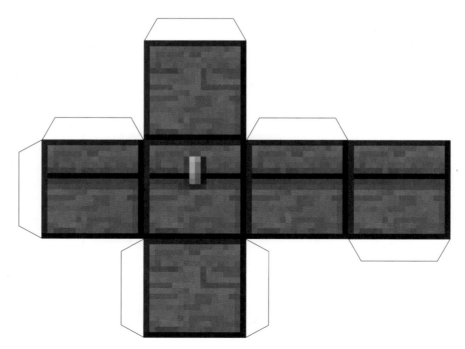

her

Trace the word below. Say the word as you trace it.

her her her her her

Finish the sentence. Write the word on the line.

She attacked the llama, so it spit at _____ .

Circle the correct word:

her   heer   here   herr   he

Color the llama.

who

Trace the word below. Say the word as you trace it.

who who who who who

Finish the sentence. Write the word on the line.

I know _____ lives in this hut.

Circle the correct word:

woo   **hoo**   **whu**

    how   **who**

Draw a picture of a witch's hut below.

would

Trace the word below. Say the word as you trace it.

would would would would

Finish the sentence. Write the word on the line.

If I had wheat, the sheep _____ follow me.

Circle the correct word:

wood   **wuld**   **would**   **wuod**   **wud**

Connect the dots to make a woolly Minecraft animal.

am

Trace the word below. Say the word as you trace it.

am   am   am   am   am

Finish the sentence. Write the word on the line.

I _____ in

the snowy tundra.

Circle the correct word:

amm   an   aim

alm   am

Solve the maze and make a sight word.

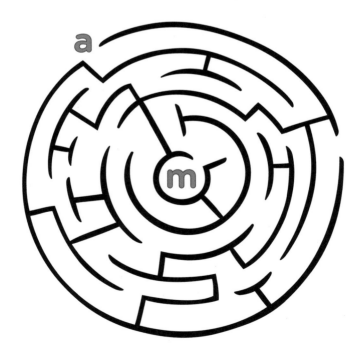

a

m

make

Trace the word below. Say the word as you trace it.

Finish the sentence. Write the word on the line.

I can _____

mushroom stew.

Circle the correct word:

meke   make   maak

      meak   mak

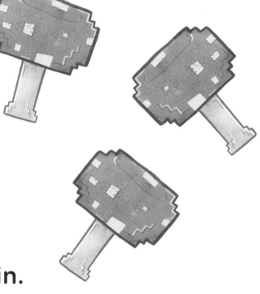

Copy the picture and color it in.

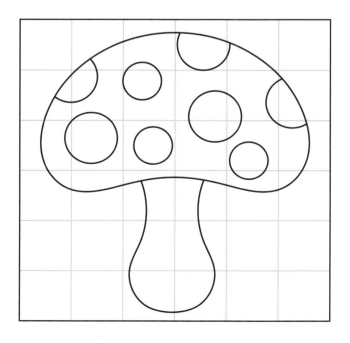
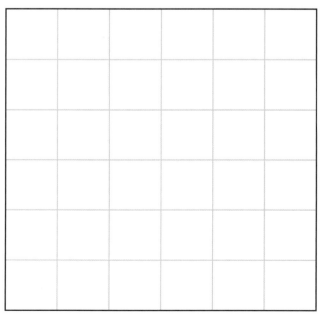

its

Trace the word below. Say the word as you trace it.

its   its   its   its   its

Finish the sentence. Write the word on the line.

The blaze shot _____ fireballs.

Circle the correct word:

itz   itt   its   sit   tis

Build the word using Minecraft blocks.

Example:

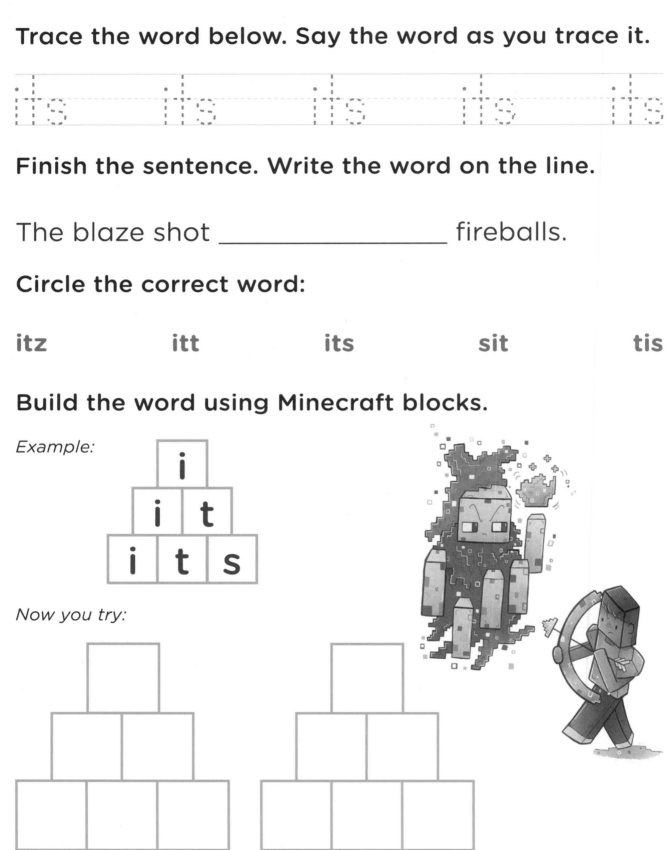

```
    i
  i   t
i   t   s
```

Now you try:

like

Trace the word below. Say the word as you trace it.

like   like   like   like   like

Finish the sentence. Write the word on the line.

I _____ to enchant weapons.

Circle the correct word:

lyke   like   lik   liek   leik

Color the trident. Add purple to enchant it.

now

Trace the word below. Say the word as you trace it.

now now now now now

Finish the sentence. Write the word on the line.

What will the angry pufferfish

do _____ ?

Circle the correct word:

new   no   won

          now   nov

Solve the maze and make a sight word.

him

Trace the word below. Say the word as you trace it.

him   him   him   him   him

Finish the sentence. Write the word on the line.

I showed _____ how to make a mob farm.

Circle the correct word:

hum   **himm**   **hin**   **hi**   **him**

Build the word using Minecraft blocks.

Example:

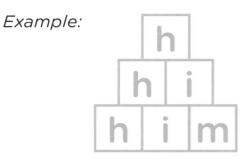

Now you try:

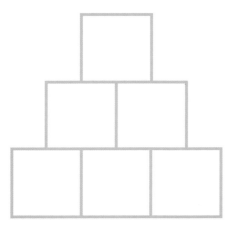 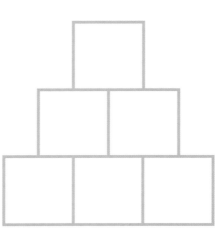

find

Trace the word below. Say the word as you trace it.

find find find find find

Finish the sentence. Write the word on the line.

Alex's cat can always

_____ her.

Circle the correct word:

fine   find   fynd

fend   fund

Connect the dots to make a tamed cat.

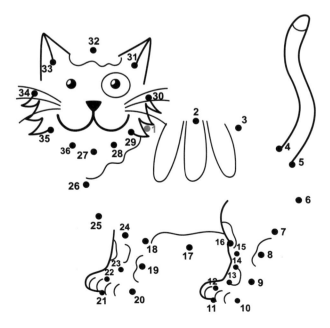

into

Trace the word below. Say the word as you trace it.

into into into into into

Finish the sentence. Write the word on the line.

The lava poured _____ the bucket.

Circle the correct word:

int   into   inot   nito   innto

Copy the picture of the bucket. To fill it with lava, color the inside orange.

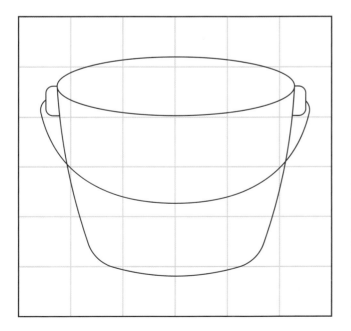 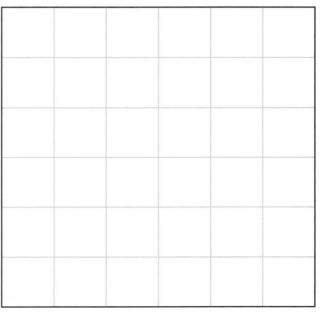

long

Trace the word below. Say the word as you trace it.

Finish the sentence. Write the word on the line.

That was a _____

way to jump.

Circle the correct word:

log   lung   long

     loog   lang

Connect the dots to make the first letter of **long**.

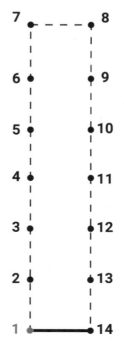

7 •----• 8
6 •   • 9
5 •   • 10
4 •   • 11
3 •   • 12
2 •   • 13
1 •———• 14

time

Trace the word below. Say the word as you trace it.

time time time time time

Finish the sentence. Write the word on the line.

The sun tells me the _____ of the day.

Circle the correct word:

time   tyme   tim   teim   itme

Draw a picture that shows a time of day in Minecraft.

has

Trace the word below. Say the word as you trace it.

Finish the sentence. Write the word on the line.

Steve _____ a potion for the zombie.

Circle the correct word:

haz   **hats**   **has**   **hass**   **his**

Build the word using Minecraft blocks.

Example:

Now you try:

day

Trace the word below. Say the word as you trace it.

day   day   day   day   day

Finish the sentence. Write the word on the line.

A _____ in Minecraft lasts for ten minutes.

Circle the correct word:

dai   da   daye   day   dad

Solve the maze and make a sight word.

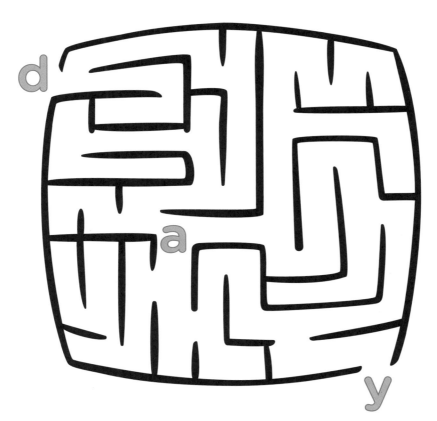

look

Trace the word below. Say the word as you trace it.

Finish the sentence. Write the word on the line.

Try not to _____

at the Endermen.

Circle the correct word:

look   lok   lock

loot   looke

Trace and color the picture of the worst weather for an Enderman.

did

Trace the word below. Say the word as you trace it.

did   did   did   did   did

Finish the sentence. Write the word on the line.

I saw the wither before he _____ .

Circle the correct word:

didd   dib   did   bid   ded

Build the word using Minecraft blocks.

Example:

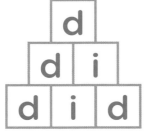

Now you try:

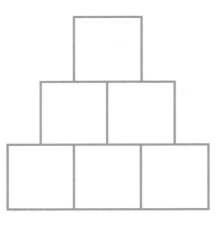
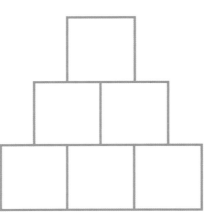

two

Trace the word below. Say the word as you trace it.

Finish the sentence. Write the word on the line.

I place _____

sticks on my crafting table.

Circle the correct word:

too   **to**   **tow**

          ton   **two**

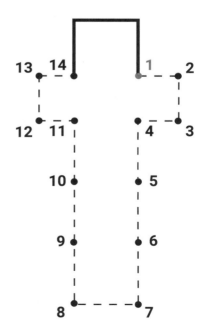

Connect the dots to make the first letter of two.

get

Trace the word below. Say the word as you trace it.

get   get   get   get   get

Finish the sentence. Write the word on the line.

I go to the Nether to _____ blaze rods.

Circle the correct word:

get   git   gete   gett   ghet

Build the word using Minecraft blocks.

Example:

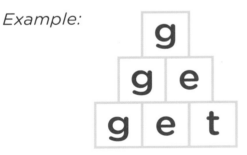

Now you try:

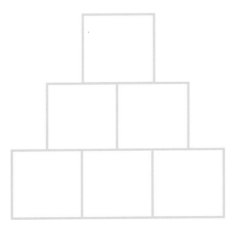
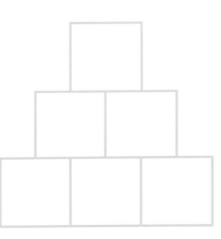

more

Trace the word below. Say the word as you trace it.

more more more more

Finish the sentence. Write the word on the line.

I need _____ gold ingots.

Circle the correct word:

mor   moir   more

moon   mote

Draw something you can craft from gold ingots.

come

Trace the word below. Say the word as you trace it.

come come come come

Finish the sentence. Write the word on the line.

Zombies _____ out when it is dark.

Circle the correct word:

com   comm   cone   come   coem

Trace and color this animal that baby zombies can ride in Minecraft.

write

Trace the word below. Say the word as you trace it.

write write write write

Finish the sentence. Write the word on the line.

I can _____ a

story about Minecraft.

Circle the correct word:

writ   rite   write

wright   wryt

Write the first sentence of a funny story about Minecraft.

_____

_____

_____

_____

made

Trace the word below. Say the word as you trace it.

made made made made

Finish the sentence. Write the word on the line.

Look at the beacon I _____ .

Circle the correct word:

mayd   maid   maed   made   mad

Build the word using Minecraft blocks.

Example:

Now you try:

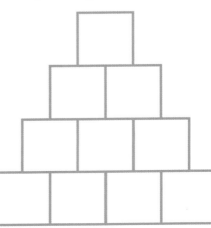   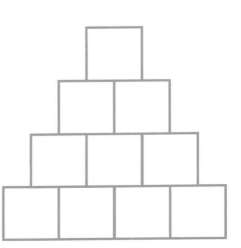

go

Trace the word below. Say the word as you trace it.

go   go   go   go   go

Finish the sentence. Write the word on the line.

I need to _____ before
I take too much damage.

Circle the correct word:

go   goe   goes

goo   got

Solve the maze and make a sight word.

g   o

may

Trace the word below. Say the word as you trace it.

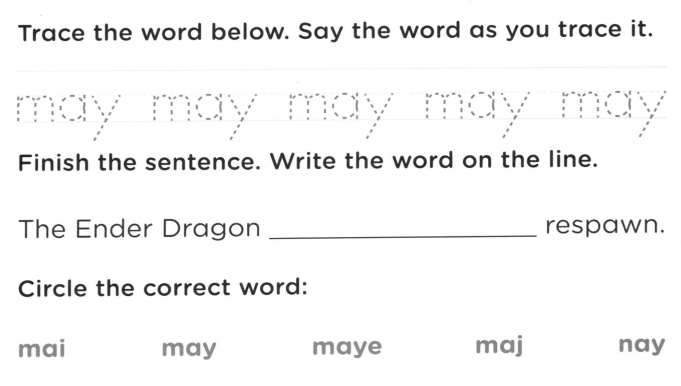

may may may may may

Finish the sentence. Write the word on the line.

The Ender Dragon _____ respawn.

Circle the correct word:

mai   may   maye   maj   nay

Color the picture of the dragon.

see

Trace the word below. Say the word as you trace it.

Finish the sentence. Write the word on the line.

I _____ a chicken jockey!

Circle the correct word:

sei   **si**   **sec**   **see**   **sea**

Build the word using Minecraft blocks.

Example:

Now you try:

part

Trace the word below. Say the word as you trace it.

Finish the sentence. Write the word on the line.

The best _____ of my day is when I play Minecraft.

Circle the correct word:

parth   pat   parr   parc   part

Draw the best part of your day below.

STEVE'S SIGHT WORD REVIEW

Practice reading and reviewing each of the 100 sight words you learned. For every word you read correctly, check the box!

☐ and   ☐ one   ☐ all   ☐ with

☐ be   ☐ had   ☐ it   ☐ use

☐ can   ☐ a   ☐ were   ☐ his

☐ down   ☐ by   ☐ he   ☐ an

☐ the   ☐ words   ☐ we   ☐ they

☐ people   ☐ in   ☐ when   ☐ each

☐ for   ☐ but   ☐ your   ☐ which

☐ I   ☐ is   ☐ on   ☐ at

☐ that   ☐ not   ☐ are   ☐ she

☐ was   ☐ you   ☐ said   ☐ do

☐ or   ☐ what   ☐ as   ☐ this

☐ of   ☐ to   ☐ there   ☐ how

- [ ] have
- [ ] their
- [ ] from
- [ ] if
- [ ] will
- [ ] number
- [ ] up
- [ ] no
- [ ] other
- [ ] way
- [ ] about
- [ ] could
- [ ] out
- [ ] these
- [ ] many

- [ ] my
- [ ] then
- [ ] first
- [ ] water
- [ ] than
- [ ] them
- [ ] so
- [ ] been
- [ ] some
- [ ] called
- [ ] her
- [ ] who
- [ ] would
- [ ] am
- [ ] make

- [ ] its
- [ ] like
- [ ] now
- [ ] him
- [ ] find
- [ ] into
- [ ] long
- [ ] time
- [ ] has
- [ ] day
- [ ] look
- [ ] did
- [ ] two
- [ ] get
- [ ] more

- [ ] come
- [ ] write
- [ ] made
- [ ] go
- [ ] may
- [ ] see
- [ ] part

THE AMAZING SIGHT WORD SEARCH

```
W  H  I  S  J  M  X  Z  G  Y  D  L  S  N  N  J  B
I  O  D  T  W  L  P  M  B  J  T  I  H  D  T  Y  L
T  N  K  O  H  H  C  Z  U  J  H  C  R  L  Z  G  V
H  N  V  T  J  E  E  A  T  T  I  B  W  Y  N  R  D
P  E  O  P  L  E  R  N  N  H  U  D  B  A  B  M  B
B  E  G  M  N  A  V  E  W  O  T  W  R  D  S  E  Y
N  T  O  L  K  N  J  V  Y  B  M  K  J  S  S  L  D
N  O  T  L  P  G  R  L  M  M  D  R  D  U  T  W  N
N  R  L  E  N  R  J  Z  V  F  U  R  Z  T  T  I  H
Z  T  H  L  W  N  Y  G  R  O  O  L  M  A  H  C  V
A  S  T  M  P  S  Z  N  Y  W  J  R  H  H  A  E  D
L  J  J  E  A  Z  S  A  I  D  M  T  D  E  O  I  Y
L  O  V  I  T  R  D  L  D  J  N  N  Y  D  N  W  T
W  A  N  S  D  R  T  A  E  O  W  W  E  R  E  J  K
H  T  A  E  X  A  H  O  N  W  D  E  W  M  X  V
B  Q  Q  R  H  X  T  N  R  F  N  N  H  M  Q  Q  N
M  D  V  W  E  D  K  G  D  A  N  X  E  T  Y  J  Y
```

AND	OR	HAD	NOT	IT	ARE	HIS	THIS
BE	OF	BY	YOU	ON	USE	AN	HOW
CAN	ONE	AT	HE	AS	YOUR	DO	HAVE
THE	FOR	IN	WE	WERE	SAID	SHE	WHICH
DOWN	THAT	IS	TO	WHAT	THERE	THEY	WORDS
PEOPLE	WAS	BUT	ALL	WHEN	WITH	EACH	

CROSSWORD FOR CRAFTERS
SIGHT WORD REVIEW

ACROSS

1. THEM
3. ABOUT
6. SOME
7. BEEN
9. THESE
10. FROM
12. WATER
15. THAN
16. NUMBER
17. COULD
21. WRITE

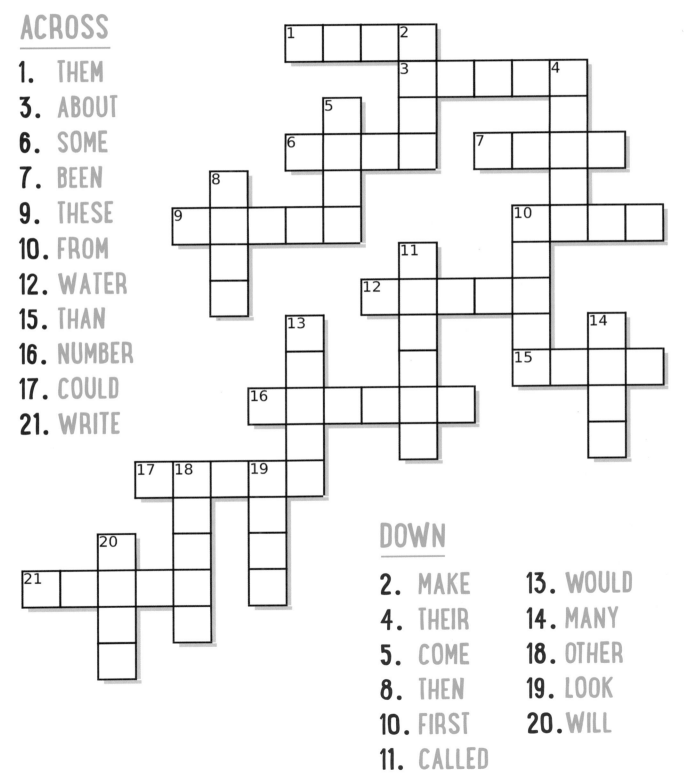

DOWN

2. MAKE
4. THEIR
5. COME
8. THEN
10. FIRST
11. CALLED

13. WOULD
14. MANY
18. OTHER
19. LOOK
20. WILL

ANSWER KEY

PAGE 4

PAGE 9

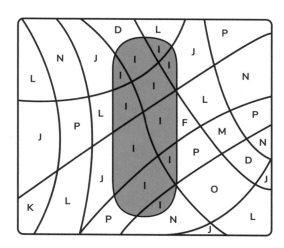

PAGE 10

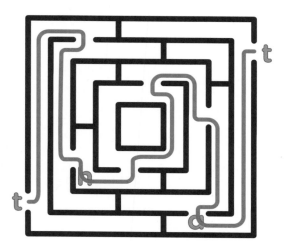

PAGE 14

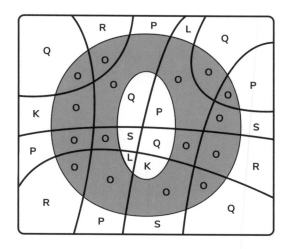

PAGE 16

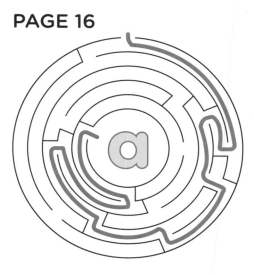

PAGE 21

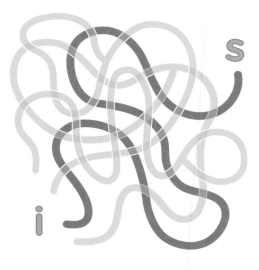

PAGE 24

PAGE 34

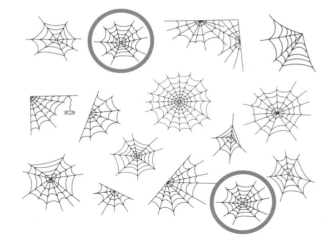

PAGE 27

PAGE 37

PAGE 33

PAGE 40

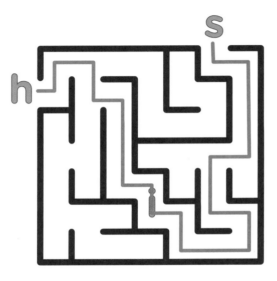

PAGE 44

PAGE 46

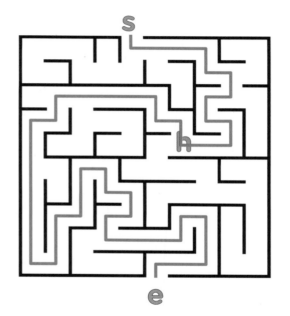

PAGE 47

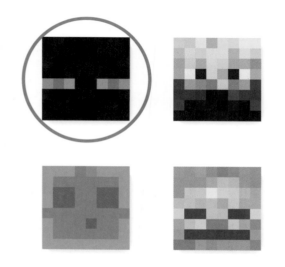

PAGE 53

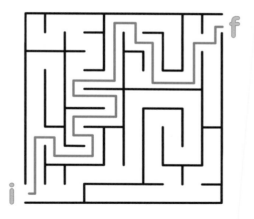

PAGE 55

PAGE 62

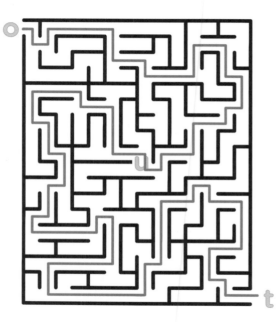

PAGE 65

PAGE 71

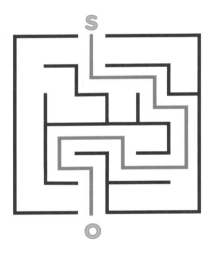

PAGE 78

PAGE 82

PAGE 89

PAGE 98

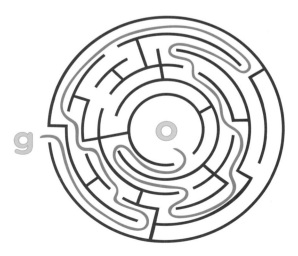

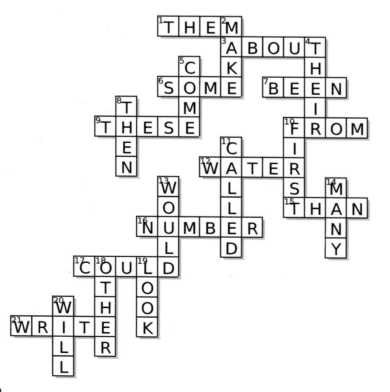